Debt Buster: Free Yourself From The Shackles In Less Than A Year

Standalone Self-Help Books

Paul Haedo

Published by Solan Publishing, 2021.

DEBT BUSTER: FREE YOURSELF FROM THE SHACKLES IN LESS THAN A YEAR

First edition. September 8, 2021.

ISBN: 979-8201029364

Written by Paul Haedo.

Also by Paul Haedo

Peacekeeper Series
Peacekeeper: Prequel
Peacekeeper
Rising Tide
Star Rising
Star Destroyer

Proletarian Hearts Series
Proletarian Hearts: Part One

Sci-Fi Box Sets
Sci-Fi Novel Mega Pack: Five Standalone Stories
Peacekeeper: The Complete Series

Standalone Erotic Stories
Innocent Pilgrim

Standalone Literary Novels
Scandinavian Tequila: A Novel

Standalone Poetry Anthologies

Haedian Poetry: Volume One

Moments Are Butterflies: A Poetry Collection

Standalone Religion, Philosophy, and Politics Books

The Communist Republic

A Dalliance Across Thought

The Word Of Era

A Man's Guide To Surviving Marriage In The 21st Century

Marxist-Haedoism

White Assimilation

Peaceful Resistance

The Reality

Standalone Romance Novels

The Director

A Chance Encounter

Beauty Unexpected

Standalone Sci-Fi Novels

Future's Guardian

Journey Home

The Designer

Pulses

World Engine

The Mycelial Invasion

Emily Reed And The Humans

Standalone Sci-Fi Short Story Anthologies
Haedian Sci-Fi Short Stories: Volume One
Haedian Sci-Fi Short Stories: Volume Two

Standalone Self-Help Books
Stack It Tall: A Guide To Writing
Debt Buster: Free Yourself From The Shackles In Less Than A Year

Watch for more at https://books2read.com/ap/n7evX1.

Table of Contents

Introduction

This book exists for just a single purpose: to show you, the reader, how to get out of debt quickly and effectively. The timeframe that we will use often throughout this book is a year; however, in most cases, the advice that will be shared with you will allow you to lift the burdens of debt on a timescale much quicker than that.

Financial literacy is, unfortunately, something that is rarely taught in school. This is unfortunate because it not only allows for the continuation of unwise decisions that result in you entering into a state of indebtedness in the first place, but it also gives debt a sort of 'supervillain' aura that it does not deserve.

Whatever the situation you currently find yourself in, always remember that there is a way out. It certainly does not seem that way now; all that you can see is the total balance growing larger and larger, but there is a way out; there always is, and there will always be. Keep this in mind as you continue to read this book: you will get out of debt's shackles; never let anyone or anything tell you otherwise.

If there is nothing else that you remember from this book, remember this: you will get through this; you will get rid of your debt. There is always a way. Never forget it, no matter what others may say or how things may seem.

Sit Down and Take a Breath

The very first thing that I want you to do is sit down and take a breath. This is the foundation of your debt-busting strategy; without it, nothing else matters. One can never formulate a plan, a strategy, or a means of attack if you are panicked and thinking illogically. Since only you, the reader, know the entirety of your present situation, it is up to you to take the first step on your path to freedom from debt. Whatever you are doing right now, sit down.

Once you are seated, no matter how high your present level of stress and worry is, take a breath. In and out. Is there anything different? Take another breath; how about now? As you read these words, imagine yourself relaxing. Do not try to ignore completely the nagging sensation of dread that you currently have; it is, after all, in your best interest to acknowledge its existence. But keep it in the back of your mind. It is alright to acknowledge its existence, but do not make it the cornerstone of your thoughts.

Now that your mind is at least partially clear, we can move on and begin the lessons that this chapter will teach you. The first lesson is another fundamental that should never be ignored or neglected: have a plan and stick to it. The plan does not have to be permanent; things always change in life, and it is rare for a plan to survive first contact with an adversary. But you need a plan, a strategy, a roadmap that tells you step by step the appropriate actions that you should take and when to take them.

If you do not have a plan, then you will waste time, money, and effort taking random jabs at your current debt load. For example, you may pay a decent chunk of your debt today, only to forget about it for the next few payment cycles. You may think that you are doing something good; after all, you paid down your debt, isn't that the point? But that action, in nearly all cases, is a poor one. By paying a chunk off and ignoring it, you can easily find yourself in the same spot as you were before.

But I paid it down! You did, but you may now have late fees, interest, and other nasty surprises that will help to balloon the balance back up. That money, more or less, was wasted since you are at the same level as before. Of course, you are better off than you would have been had you never paid the lump sum in the first place, but you still have a total debt balance, and the balance is still the same amount as it was before.

However, if you had a carefully researched and detailed plan, things might have gone differently. For example, if your interest rate is low, but the penalties for making late payments or skipping payments are high, you are better off making sure that you make payments every billing cycle and never miss a single one than if you make a large payment and then ignore several billing cycles before making another payment. This is where having a plan truly shines because you can take the interest rates that your debt has, and the respective late fees and penalties that you may incur if you miss a payment, and mathematically come up with the best repayment strategy for your debt.

For example, if your interest rate is incredibly low, say 1%-2%, then the debt is something that the traditional advice of paying it off every month as much as you can easily rectifies. If the interest rate is much higher, say 10%-20%, then the same premise applies; however, it is in your best interest to get rid of the debt amount as quickly as possible. This is where strategies such as refinancing come into play. If you understand the terms of your debt, then you can begin to form a strategy to get yourself out of it.

For example, if you have the option to get yourself a loan of, say, $20,000 at a 2% interest rate while you currently have a debt total of $15,000 at a 15% interest rate, then the best course of action for you is to take that loan at 2%. You are, for a brief moment, almost doubling your total debt balance, but you can then use $15,000 of the 2% loan to completely pay off the 15% loan, with $5,000 remaining. You can then use the remaining $5,000 to pay off a portion of the $20,000 loan at 2%. You will then have $15,000 in debt, the exact same amount that you had previously.

But there is a major difference: instead of a 15% interest rate, you now have a 2% interest rate. You are in the same position as before, but you suddenly made the road ahead much easier. That is the benefit of sitting down and taking a breath; you can see the options that are currently available to you, and you can form a plan to get yourself out of debt. Had you not taken the time to sit down and calmly go over your available options, there is a good chance that you would have missed the above option. After all, going into more debt to make getting out of debt easier is not exactly the most obvious thing.

That is all for this chapter. Remember, reader, the very first thing that you should do is sit down and take a breath. Everything else that this book teaches you will be useless to you in your quest to get out of debt if you neglect to do so. Debt, and those who benefit from your indebtedness, want nothing more than for you to continue to run around like a headless chicken, utterly terrified and scared of what the future may hold. Do not give them a second longer of satisfaction; sit down and take a breath. You now know that there is a way out, and the first step is to take a breath and calm down.

Make A Plan

We have alluded to this in the previous chapter, but the very next thing that you want to do, after you have taken a seat and calmed yourself down, is to plan. Everyone knows the basics of planning, and we have already touched on those in the last chapter. Thus, in this chapter, we will discuss what your plan should contain in order to be most useful to you in your quest to break the debt load that is currently keeping you down.

The very first element of a successful debt-busting plan is knowledge. Most specifically, you want to obtain as much knowledge pertaining to your debt terms as you can. Luckily, in order to enforce debt and collect upon it, the entity in question that issued it will provide you with a contract in which all the terms and conditions are mentioned. Most skim over the terms and conditions; in your case, you want to sit down and read through it all. Photocopy the contract if you do not already have copies, and then grab a pen or highlighter.

Once you have in hand a copy of the contract that lays out the terms of your debt, highlight particularly important information. This will be anything that pertains to interest rates and how the interest rate is calculated. For example, is the 2% interest rate added to the total balance every month, every year, or is it added on a sliding scale, and so on? In addition to anything involving the interest rate, look for fee clauses: do you incur a fee if you make a late payment, or do you just need to worry about interest?

All of these things you want to figure out because they are vital in determining the best course of action going forward. Once you have the vital information regarding your debt accessible, you want to begin to modify the foundational strategy of your plan in such a way as to best counter the terms of your debt. We will discuss all of these different strategies in greater detail in future chapters, but for now, keep them in mind as you begin to form your debt-busting plan.

For example, if your debt has high interest, you should pay down the amount as much as possible or even get yourself into further debt at a lower interest rate in order to wipe the higher debt off and only have lower interest debt to deal with.

If, on the other hand, it is low interest but has high fees for late and delayed payments, then you want to figure out, firstly, the size of the debt and whether or not you should even attempt to pay it down, instead of seeking an alternative method for getting rid of the total balance, such as bankruptcy.

Finally, look at the impact of debt in terms of opportunity cost. Opportunity cost will be the topic of our next chapter, but it is one of the most important things that you need to keep in mind as you begin to decide the best course forward as you deal with your debt. Every action in the financial world has an opportunity cost; money spent, after all, is money that you no longer have for other things. This is why you should get in the habit of forming plans before spending money, not only to get out of debt but also to avoid it as much as you can in the future.

Remember that you are not responsible nor at fault for your current situation. The previous you, who exists in the past, is someone that no longer exists, and the future you, who will exist in the future, is someone whose characteristics you alone can control through the actions and thoughts that you have in the present. Lots of people want to blame the individual who has debt; it is a strategy that is convenient. "Oh, you are responsible for the mess that you are currently in," "Only a deadbeat walks away from his debts." On and on the blame will come; you need to ignore it.

Debt can, and often does, occur to those who had no intention of entering it in the first place. The majority of debt occurs because of events that are outside one's control: healthcare costs, college costs, unexpected expenses that exceed the money reserves that one currently has; the list of things that cause unexpected debt is endless. Never forget, as you make your plan, that you do not owe anyone any sort of comfort regarding their moral opinion. Focus exclusively on getting out of debt.

Keep In Mind the Opportunity Cost

We have briefly mentioned this near the end of the previous chapter, but the opportunity cost of your financial decisions regarding debt is something that you should always have in the back of your mind. Each payment, each decision, all adds up to a result. And each open door that you walk through as you make a decision will result in several other doors closing. You cannot make every single possible decision; the very act of making a certain decision will prevent you from making another decision, all because of the opportunity cost.

For example, we have the strategy of bankruptcy. We will cover bankruptcy in the next chapter in greater detail, but for now, bankruptcy is a perfect example to help illustrate opportunity cost. Bankruptcy, depending on the type of bankruptcy that you end up filing, can either completely alleviate your total debt obligation or allow you to repay it over an extended period of time, whether it be the complete balance or just a partial balance. There are other forms of bankruptcy, but all forms more or less exist to help protect a debtor, also known as you, from facing a situation where they can never hope to get out of debt.

There, however, is an opportunity cost to bankruptcy. In many cases, for several years, your access to credit is more or less denied. If you do end up obtaining access to credit, usually it is on terms that can be considered predatory. For example, you may face sky-high interest rates, minimum payment clauses (you must pay a minimum of 30 payments before you can fully pay off the debt, etc.), and other such clauses that serve to completely skew the balance of power in the financial relationship over to the party that issues the debt. That is why, for all intents and purposes, your access to credit after bankruptcy is more or less denied.

You also lose your assets in the event that the bankruptcy completely discharges your debt obligation, or in the event that you face a repayment plan form of bankruptcy, you lose control until the court-ordered repayment plan is completed. All possible economic opportunities that may be available to you in the future will be closed off until either your access to credit is regained or the repayment plan that was ordered by the bankruptcy court is completed. This is an opportunity cost that you need to keep in mind.

In addition to bankruptcy, there are other strategies that we will discuss later on in this book that also have immense opportunity costs. For example, following the chapter on bankruptcy, we have the chapter on fleeing the country. This is a strategy that is especially effective in the event of debt that cannot be discharged in bankruptcy, such as tax debt, student loan debt in the case of the United States, or child support and other family law debts, as well as standard court judgments enacted against the loser in a court case.

Opportunity costs here are somewhat obvious; if you leave the country in order to escape the painful burden of debt, then the opportunity cost is the great difficulty in returning. Your life in the country in which you currently reside is more or less over, and you have to be willing to leave things behind that matter in more ways than just money. For example, the opportunity cost of not being able to attend the funeral of a relative or rarely, if ever, seeing a grandchild from one of your kids—these are opportunity costs that you need to keep in mind. Then again, if you fail to pay your debt and end up in jail, you will have the same opportunity cost as fleeing the country, so the choice sometimes can be obvious, albeit forced.

Bankruptcy

We are now ready to discuss in detail specific strategies related to busting your debt. The timeframe that we will keep in mind throughout this book is a year or less in terms of implementing said strategies, but for many of these strategies, they can be done in much less time. We start with arguably the most important decision that anyone who wishes to get out of debt will face: "Do I declare bankruptcy, or do I pay back the debt?"

This is a very important decision, one that should not be taken lightly, much less rushed. Most guides to getting out of debt skip over bankruptcy completely. They mention the 'moral consequences,' the 'economic consequences that last for years,' and then move on without another word on the matter. Not only is this a disservice to the reader of said guide, but it is a terrible piece of advice to give to someone who wants to get out of debt. There are two foundational paths to getting out of debt: bankruptcy and paying off the debt through the use of currency.

To neglect to teach about bankruptcy is to ignore half of the curriculum. Morals, quite frankly, are a luxury—one of the many luxuries enjoyed by those who do not have the axe of debt hanging over their heads.

Thus, we begin. First and foremost, to determine whether you should pursue bankruptcy or not, you will need to sit down and carefully analyze your current financial situation. The same process that you use to formulate a plan and strategy regarding your debt is what you want to use to determine whether or not bankruptcy is the correct path.

Before you begin to analyze the terms of your debt, you want to see the respective position that your broader life is currently in. What kind of opportunities do you see coming your way? Of these opportunities, how many will involve the necessity of having good credit? Do you plan on marrying a spouse, mortgaging property, or investing in a new business enterprise? All of these questions should be asked and answered.

For example, if you plan on doing all of the above, then bankruptcy can present significant problems. If you are married or planning to be married, your spouse may not view your plans for bankruptcy in a positive light. Remember that bankruptcy is one of the 'taboos' of society. There is a reason why some financial literacy guides go to great lengths to avoid the subject. Especially in nations where the economic markets are broad and highly competitive, bankruptcy is intertwined with the religious morals of society and is viewed as a sin.

Because of this, your spouse may not want to marry a 'deadweight,' 'loser,' 'deadbeat,' etc. Of course, if your spouse would rather have you suffer under debt in order to keep up appearances instead of declaring bankruptcy, one can easily make the argument that marrying such a person is unwise. However, marriage advice is a complicated topic that lies far outside the scope of this book, and thus we move on.

If you are looking to mortgage property or have access to a line of credit for a new business enterprise, then bankruptcy will more or less put such ambitions on hold for at least half a decade or more. Lenders will be fearful of you, not just because of the 'inherent risk' of default that you pose, but because you are willing to declare bankruptcy in the first place! After all, if you have no issue with using the full power of the judicial system for your interests, then you are someone who cannot be conned into paying off unreasonable debts because 'it is the right and moral thing to do.'

It seems that the price of bankruptcy is steep, but now we get to the benefits, which are enormous. First and foremost, bankruptcy gives you the power to walk away. This is something that seems obvious but is often ignored. The debt burden that you currently have, the burden that you are reading this book in order to learn how to get rid of? Bankruptcy makes it go poof, and if it does not, allows you to greatly weaken it with a court-approved repayment plan. It is the ultimate shortcut to getting rid of your debt.

Returning to the subject of whether you should declare bankruptcy or not, now that you have asked yourself the respective questions of opportunity cost and future goals, you should begin to ask yourself questions regarding the debt that you currently have. How large is the total outstanding balance? What is the interest rate? What are the respective fees, and when do they come into play? This, combined with the questions of opportunity cost and future goals, will give you the answer as to whether you should pursue bankruptcy or not.

Bankruptcy tends to work exceptionally well for debts that are sudden, unavoidable, and a result of events outside of your control. Debts incurred because of medical costs, for example, are perfect candidates for bankruptcy, not only because they meet all three of the above conditions, but also because the sums tend to be astronomical if you do not have insurance or a governmental program that can cover the expense. If you start with a principal that rivals the total cost of a house, then there is no reason other than idiocy for not declaring bankruptcy.

Of course, the dilemma of losing everything that you own is present, and here is where we start to enter into very morally murky territory. To help make navigating such murky waters somewhat easier, let us continue with the example of medical debt that we have mentioned above. Let us say that you have recently suffered a medical event, perhaps an illness that needed a great deal of medicine and medical care in order to overcome, or an accident that caused major damage to your mind and body.

You now have a total debt amount to the tune of several hundred thousand dollars, a figure that will likely take you several decades to repay on your current wage and salary. Perhaps you are already in middle age, and very quickly you see that you will be lucky to repay this debt by the time that you die. Furthermore, you do not know if you may need further medical treatment in the future; your medical event may return, or you may suffer another medical event that will definitely ensure that you never repay the debt that you owe as long as you live. To add insult to injury, the hospitals where you stayed want the full balance and will not reduce it.

Now, most people will say that this is a wholly unacceptable situation and that bankruptcy was 'designed' for such cases. Clearly, the debt was a result of something that could not be blamed on the individual. The debt was not taken willingly; it was taken because the medical care was necessary to avoid an early death. This allows for the usual suspects who whine about 'personal responsibility' to either keep their mouths shut or join in with regards to supporting the decision to declare bankruptcy.

No one disagrees with this, but here is where the waters start to suddenly get murky. Bankruptcy will wipe out all your assets and financial reserves, as well as all of your debts. Your slate is wiped clean; the medical debt of several hundred thousand dollars is cleared, but so is everything else. Priceless heirlooms that have been in the family for generations? They are to be sold at auction, and the proceeds given to the lenders. What about the money in the bank account that was to be a down payment on a house? Gone, wired straight to the bank accounts of the lenders.

We can clearly see that this situation is unfair. You did everything right; you saved your money, you avoided frivolous debt that occurs when you try to live outside of your means. You worked hard at your job, and you are a responsible citizen. But no matter how many times you try to talk to the lenders from the various hospitals, they will not budge. "You earn too much for need-based aid," "Your treatment was very expensive," and on and on. Thus, we are now in the murky waters.

Why are the waters murky? Because you are so frustrated with the lenders and their lack of compassion and humanity that you end up deciding that you do not want to give them a single penny. You decide to conceal some of your assets in order to have a nest egg to bounce back with once your debt is cleared. You decide to liquidate most of your money and convert it into cash. You then head to a famous gambling area and proceed to 'lose' it all in a glorious display of sadness, despair, and frustration. You were not thinking clearly after all; you were depressed and in despair, thinking that your life was over.

Of course, in reality, you maybe lost a few thousand dollars at most. The rest you converted into assets that are rich in value and easy to transport and conceal, such as gold. Fifty or so gold coins can easily reach a value of a hundred thousand dollars, all the money that you have managed to save up over years of hard work and toil. Now destitute, you return home, hide the coins in a location that no one other than you will find, and you try to keep your head above water for several months.

Once it becomes clear that you simply cannot continue to live with the debt load that you have, you file for bankruptcy. The lawyers for the hospitals grill you on your 'gambling' event, demanding to see receipts and bank transactions. You show them the massive bank transactions right before you went off to blow it all away on gambling. "I just wanted to bet it all and win enough money to get out of the debt that I was in." That is your rebuttal to each and every question that the lender lawyers ask. You tried to recover, but you could not. There is no bank record of you buying gold because you paid for it in cash, and the money trail stops at the withdrawals, with you spending the last of your bank deposits on hotels near the casinos.

On paper, your story checks out, and even with a warrant to search your home, something that the lender lawyers pushed for, nothing was found. You 'pawned' your heirlooms away, and the few meager possessions that you had were liquidated by the bankruptcy court and the funds given to the hospital lenders. Your debt is purged, and you very slowly sell off your gold coins. For all intents and purposes, the new business that you just opened seems to be rich and vibrant in luck and profit.

Now that the little story that was shared above has ended, we are presented with a dilemma. The individual in question above committed a crime; they omitted from the bankruptcy court assets that they owned. Of course, the 'crime' was done in such a way that it was almost impossible to prove. Unless the bank lawyers manage to obtain evidence linking you to gold merchants, there is no evidence that the money had not actually been lost in gambling. And even if they manage to obtain evidence that links you to gold merchants, you can just say that you lost the gold that you purchased in a moment of drunken confusion.

Such moral dilemmas will pop up all the time in your journey towards getting rid of your debt. The upcoming chapter titled "Fleeing The Country" is going to be filled with them. But they are dilemmas that you need to seriously consider, because, as I said previously, morals, quite frankly, are a luxury; one of the many luxuries that are enjoyed by those who do not have the axe of debt hanging over their heads.

This is why bankruptcy is such a taboo, and why many books that teach how to get out of debt do their best to skim over the topic of bankruptcy before moving on and forgetting all about it. It is a taboo because it encourages you to view debt as a chain around your neck, a chain that should be broken and removed as soon as possible. Once you see that debt itself tends to grow into a beast that is many times its original size, you start to get some 'ideas' about preserving your own wealth through bankruptcy, especially when you start to view the system as inherently unfair to the person who is suffering from debt.

Some areas are fairer than others; for example, there are certain states in the United States that will allow you to exempt certain essential assets from bankruptcy, such as a 'homestead' house and vehicle. In such areas, the above story would be foolish and unnecessary, since the hundred-thousand-dollar reserve that the individual had accumulated over years of hard work could be funneled into equity in the homestead. Since the homestead is exempt from bankruptcy proceedings, the wealth is more or less stored in the house, in the form of equity and not gold coins that are secretly hidden.

In conclusion, bankruptcy is a strategy that effectively cleans the entire plate; all of the good and all of the bad are removed. The disgusting insect that just jumped onto the plate is removed, but so is the juicy and tender cut of meat on the opposite side, which is far away from the insect. It is the nuclear bomb of the financial world; the entire financial portfolio of the individual is blown up, allowing the individual to start anew from the very bottom. Only you can decide whether such a nuclear bomb is necessary or not, but with the information contained in this chapter and the information that will be taught to you throughout this book, you are now sufficiently prepared to decide.

Fleeing The Country

Here we jump into one of the most, if not the most, controversial 'strategies' for busting the debt that you are currently dragging. What is this incredibly taboo strategy? Fleeing the country. That is right, you get on a plane to another land, and you do not look back. Ironically enough, this can oftentimes be less illegal than the 'tell a little lie to the bankruptcy court' strategy that was mentioned in the previous chapter. It all has to do with the realities of sovereign judicial authority.

First and foremost, an explanation of sovereign judicial authority. With the exception of nations that have entered into a mutual pact with one another, which permits the judicial system of one nation to enforce decrees against inhabitants and citizens of another nation, such as the European Union, the authority of the judicial system of one respective nation begins and ends inside the borders of said nation. This is incredibly convenient and beneficial for the individual who is suffering from the burden of debt.

You see, bankruptcy, while powerful, is not the solution that solves everything. The nuclear bomb of the financial world is quite similar to the nuclear bomb of the real world; it has a purpose, but it certainly cannot be used in every single possible situation. One major issue that many who suffer from debt will face is debt that cannot be discharged in bankruptcy.

Usually, this is debt that is a result of direct judicial action. For example, if you lose a lawsuit, the entity that sued you may be awarded financial damages. These damages, for the most part, cannot be discharged in bankruptcy. If they could, then losing a lawsuit would lose most of its impact and meaning. This is a great thing when a victim seeks financial compensation from a wealthy and powerful defendant who has wronged him; not such a great thing, however, if a wealthy and powerful plaintiff sues you with a frivolous lawsuit, which somehow manages to stick thanks to sufficient legal elbow grease.

There are other judicial cases where debt cannot be discharged in bankruptcy. Another common debt that cannot be discharged in bankruptcy, and which causes many debtors to end up fleeing the country, is family court debt. This is usually in the form of alimony, child support, and other such debts. These debts exist to shield the state as much as possible from the financial consequences of divorce and procreation. Babies and young children require great financial resources to be reared into adulthood; child support is designed to ensure that these resources come from the parents instead of the state.

Alimony, on the other hand, tries to ensure that normal sacrifices incurred by the spouses in order to form a more efficient marriage and family are reimbursed and compensated. A stay-at-home parent sacrifices earning power, which needs to be compensated now that the parents have decided to break the family apart through divorce. These specific types of debt have a purpose, and it is a good purpose: to help provide for kids in the case of child support debt and to help compensate the divorced spouse for family and marriage labor that the spouse ended up sacrificing earning power to obtain.

But like all things related to debt, it is detrimental when there is too much of it. Remember the comment above about these debts existing to shield the state as much as possible from the financial consequences of divorce and procreation? Well, the state wants the total financial consequences that it has to deal with to be as close to zero as possible, which naturally means these family court debts tend to skyrocket in size in several sinister ways.

One of the most sinister ways that these types of debts tend to skyrocket is in the actual amount owed. These debts are not initial principal debts that are then paid down, with interest added after each billing cycle. Instead, these debts are more like rents upon the income that the respective individual will earn in the future. Alimony and child support are thus percentages of gross income debts. For the sake of convenience, we will say that alimony plus child support for a single-child family unit that is broken is 25% of gross income.

Not only do we have a sinister type of debt because one can never 'repay' this debt in the traditional sense, but we also have something much worse: the 'assumption' by the court that such debt will be paid. Now, before we continue, I must make it clear to the reader that the debate regarding the morals of these two types of debt is one that we will not enter.

There, after all, is a legitimate purpose as to why these types of debt are the way that they are: to provide for the fragments of the destroyed family unit, to avoid the state having to pay for the fragments of the destroyed family unit, and so on. Whether one is a 'deadbeat' for not paying these debts is irrelevant to the topic of this book, which is busting debt. However, because this particular debt cannot be 'busted' in the traditional sense, we discuss its nature first before returning to the topic of this chapter, which is fleeing the country.

Returning to the nature of this debt, the court assumes that the debtor can repay this 'rent,' or tax if you wish to view it as such. If the debtor cannot repay it, then the debtor is clearly 'refusing' to pay the debt. Again, the morality debate over whether one is a 'deadbeat' for not being able to pay the twin debts of alimony and child support is a debate that we are not entering. Let's assume for the sake of argument that the debtor is not a 'deadbeat' and is simply being assumed by the court to be in contempt of the court order out of willful refusal to pay this debt.

The family court can assume the correct income that the debtor should be paying and then use this assumption to govern the total debt that should be repaid each billing cycle. If the debt cannot be paid, penalties can be severe, up to imprisonment. Effectively, family court debt is the only type of debt that allows for debtor's prisons as a form of punishment for not paying.

Now that we have discussed family court debt as much as possible without entering the great debate that would require an entire book to settle, we return to the topic that this chapter addresses: fleeing the country. As you can see, this is a debt determined by an outside party, entirely in its own interests. If the state ends up paying for the destroyed family unit and/or children who do not have a double parental income source to rely on, then the state can determine the amount you should repay and imprison you if you cannot repay it.

Returning to the 25% of gross income example we have been discussing, let's say that you, the debtor who has to repay this family court debt, lose your means of income. Perhaps the job you have been working at has fired you or laid you off because your specific position was no longer needed. And let's assume that you cannot, for whatever reason, find a job that is similar in income level to the one you just lost.

The state continues to demand 25% of the gross income that was your old income. To pay off that 25% of the old gross, you effectively have to hand over about 90% of your current gross income. This effectively leaves you destitute because you cannot cover all the other expenses of life with just 10% remaining of your salary. You know this, but the state insists that you pay the 25% of the old gross, and if you do not, you will be imprisoned.

You sit down and take a breath, following the advice taught to you in the very first chapter of this book after the introduction. You begin to view your options, and the situation you are currently in does not look good. Firstly, you cannot declare bankruptcy. The debt you must pay to the family court cannot be discharged in bankruptcy, and even if it could, you would still have to pay 25% of your old gross income every month. You'd be destitute once again in just a few months after declaring bankruptcy.

With bankruptcy out of the picture, you try to see if you can get the court to lower the debt. The court, naturally, because it is trying to avoid burdening the state with more obligations, refuses to budge from the 25% of old gross income that is your obligation. You appeal, and the appeal is immediately shot down by the higher court. Because of this, the option of appealing the decision is out and not available to you.

Finally, you try to see if you can fix this problem by earning more income. Initially, all goes well. You earn more income, and suddenly the 25% of the old gross income does not sting that much. Unexpectedly, you get a temporary trial position for almost double your previous pay! Now the 25% of old gross income is only 12.5% of your new gross income. You rest easy, assuming that you have cleverly solved the dilemma you were in.

Naturally, for the sake of this example, such a thing is not to be. The family court gets wind of your new income, and they now impute your total debt obligation to be 25% of your current pay. You are now back to where you were previously;

however, 25% is only 25%. You still have 75% of your income to play around with, and after taxes and expenses, maybe you have 5% of your total income left to save for a rainy day.

That is until you are terminated. Remember that the position that was giving you double the income of your old job was a temporary trial position. The trial ended, and the employer decided not to keep you after the trial. Now you are more or less screwed because the 25% of your income obligation now becomes over 180% of your income obligation.

Of course, you point this out to the court and ask if they could at the very least bring the now ridiculous family court debt obligation down to what it was previously. They refuse, saying that your income potential is now what your most recently fired job had given you. You cannot declare bankruptcy, adjusting the debt total is impossible even after one last desperate appeal, and finding the equivalent of that one-in-a-million job is all but impossible.

This is your situation, and you are presented with one unfortunate truth: you cannot escape or win this situation in any way. You will be unable to pay off the debt, and you will be imprisoned for being in 'contempt' of court. There is only one thing that you can do: flee the country.

I mentioned family court debt because this is the most common of the debts that lead someone to flee the country. Another is student loan debt if you are in the United States, due to the inability to discharge it in bankruptcy. Furthermore, judgments against you by a court can also be a debt that leads you to flee the country, especially if you cannot discharge the judgment in bankruptcy and the judgment is severe enough that there is no hope of repaying it in any reasonable amount of time.

Step one in preparing to flee the country is to select a destination. This is important because each country is different and will have different immigration rules, as well as mutual judicial enforcement treaties. You, after all, do not want to flee the country only to end up in a country that accepts the judicial debts of the country you just fled from. You'd be right back at square one. You also want to avoid being deported before you are given the right to remain in the country or the right to citizenship in the new country. If you are deported back to your old country, then fleeing again will be much harder.

Once you have selected a destination, you need to find the quickest and best way to either obtain citizenship or, failing that, permanent residency. This is the most important part of fleeing the country; without official rights in the new country, there is nothing stopping your old country from putting pressure on your new country in order to deport you and send you back. Furthermore, if your old country revokes your passport—a punishment that is very common if you have large amounts of judgment or family court debt—then most visas that you may have obtained in a new country become invalid.

This is why fleeing the country is a strategy that is best prepared for during good times. The vast majority of you who are reading this book will not be facing a debt that cannot be discharged in bankruptcy or a debt that can result in imprisonment if you are unable to pay it off. Still, you never know the wild events that life can throw at you; maybe in a decade's time, you will be cursing yourself from a jail cell because you did not have a second passport in hand when you could have really used one.

Preparation for this strategy is quite simple: aim to have two citizenships at the bare minimum, three if you want to have a more or less guaranteed ability to flee the country. The great news is that obtaining multiple citizenships is very beneficial, especially in the field of business. Being able to visit a potential client in a country and not have to worry about tourist or business visas, especially if you wish to pursue a business relationship with said client if the opportunity arises, is an ability that gives you peace of mind and great fortune.

Because pursuing multiple citizenships is a strategy that acts as both insurance against debt and a powerful debt-busting strategy, we will briefly cover how to obtain them. The easiest two methods involve ancestry and marriage, in that order. Ancestry is the easiest method; you simply need to look at your lineage and obtain a few papers for this method.

Once you've confirmed your lineage to an ancestor who had the citizenship that you either want or can obtain, you then need to obtain birth certificates and other identifying documents to prove the connection between you and this ancestor. This becomes progressively harder the more generations there are between you and the ancestor. If you wish to claim citizenship by right of a parent, it is painless, and nearly all countries have provisions to allow for such a thing. If you want to claim citizenship from a great-great-grandparent, on the other hand, not only are there very few countries that will allow for such a thing to occur, but obtaining all the documents for such an endeavor will be very difficult.

That is all there is to it; hence, why it is the easiest way to obtain citizenship. You find the papers proving that you are a descendant of the ancestor, and then walk to a consulate or embassy of the nation from which you want citizenship, show the papers, and start the process of naturalization. Of course, this oftentimes does not work for everyone, especially if you are part of the European-African-Asian diaspora in the Americas or if you are an orphan. Sometimes proving descent is impossible, or one of your ancestors somehow lost citizenship before it passed down to you.

In that case, we have the second easiest method of obtaining another citizenship: marriage. It is more or less as easy as the previous method; however, the twin factors of needing to get married in the first place and then spending a trial period of a few years as a permanent resident before being awarded citizenship by the new country make it somewhat harder than obtaining citizenship through ancestry. Still, the vast majority of people will get married at least once in their lives; why not have citizenship be a benefit of that marriage? Considering that it is granted after just a few years of marriage and living in the new country, even if the marriage ends in divorce relatively quickly, you can still obtain an additional passport and additional peace of mind in case you ever need to flee a country and the debts within.

To conclude this chapter, a few options will be mentioned for the unfortunate reader who lacks a second or third passport and needs to flee the country because of unpayable debt. The circumstances for you are grim, but, as we mentioned in the introduction to this book, there is always a way, no matter how things may seem. They will be options that will require sacrifice on your part, but they are better than a lifetime of imprisonment, followed by release, begging, and then reimprisonment as you fail to pay the debt that you can never repay or discharge.

First and foremost, see if you can claim asylum or refuge in another country. Look at the countries that are on the worst terms with the country you are trying to flee from and share your story with the state news organization of the country to which you wish to flee. The propaganda and moral-boosting value of a foreign national who is willing to share the horror stories of living in the enemy country is immense, and you may be able to obtain a job as a political commentator in this new country. Of course, you will have to spend years attacking the country from which you fled in every possible way, and everyone back 'home' will call you a traitor and hate you for life, but if a debtor's prison is all that awaits you back home, it is a good trade-off.

If the above is not possible, or simply not something that you can stomach, see if you can obtain residency and then citizenship by enlisting in the armed forces of another nation. The great part about this strategy is simple: by enlisting in the armed forces of another nation, particularly if the nation is not on good terms with the nation you fled from, you, in many cases, automatically lose your citizenship from the country you fled from. It is logical: by openly fighting for another country, your loyalties to your home country will be severely damaged. Since you lose your citizenship, you can no longer be extradited for non-severe crimes, which your non-dischargeable debts fall under. And since you are fighting in the armed forces of another nation, your path to citizenship in that nation is a strong one.

Some nations allow for an easier time in enlisting in the armed forces for citizenship than others. France is one country that is arguably the best in the world for this very thing. Thanks to the French Foreign Legion, foreigners from around the world can more or less start a new life and be given citizenship and a new identity if they so choose after completing their term of service. If you are injured in battle as a French Foreign Legionnaire, you are automatically given citizenship by France. They accept all profiles, even those with non-severe criminal backgrounds, which you have.

Those are the two best ways to try to flee the country if you lack any other citizenship other than the one you currently have. All the other methods tend to result in a miserable existence; being an illegal immigrant, for example, is a fate that can be worse than imprisonment. You need the rights, benefits, and privileges that citizenship provides, especially in the modern age. Without it, you cannot work, seek healthcare through normal channels, and you will lack many basic legal rights. Then again, such assistance may be better than imprisonment; only you can answer that dilemma.

We conclude with a final point: if all else fails and you cannot flee the country, then try to put pressure on the state through lawsuits and by sharing your story far and wide in order to obtain positive public opinion. We will discuss strategies to do just that in the upcoming chapter: Suing the Issuer of the Debt, but for now, keep it in mind if all else fails.

Becoming Judgment Proof

We return now to the regular household debts that cannot be enforced through imprisonment but can still be enforced through the seizure of assets and money. This is a dual prevention/shield strategy for managing such debts, which is to become judgment proof. In certain cases, one's lifestyle leads to the accumulation of debts often enough that bankruptcy every once in a while is simply not enough to prevent them.

The reader may ask: "What kind of foolish lifestyle is this?" The answer is quite simple: many different kinds of lifestyles. In fact, any lifestyle, whether good or bad, has the potential to lead to this. The reason is quite simple, as well as sad. In all cases, debt can be fixed with an increase in income and disposable money. Debt shackles and beats you down because you lack the money to both pay it off and avoid it in the first place. While the very rich can use debt as a positive financial tool, borrowing vast sums of money against their extensive asset reserves without having to pay tax, the poor need to borrow against their future earnings for money that is desperately needed here and now to pay for vital life expenses.

Hence, the answer is many different kinds of lifestyles that can lead to the accumulation of debts often enough that bankruptcy every once in a while is simply not enough to prevent them. Trying to judge the lifestyle of the individual in order to then lay blame on said individual for being in debt is a foolish proposition in nearly all cases. Are there exceptions to this rule? Of course, there are many examples to choose from where the person is entirely at fault for the massive debts that they currently have. But in most cases, bad luck draws even worse luck, and the individual then finds themselves trapped in a massive pile of debt and fees that seem inescapable.

Returning to the topic of becoming judgment proof, we can see the same factors at play. Especially in the realm of court judgments, many who 'lose' a court case lose only because the judge and/or jury believe them to be at fault. Humans are not perfect creatures, and especially if the information that we are given is not absolute and completely true, we cannot be expected to come up with the best, fairest, and most accurate decision each and every time.

There are many things that can muddy the waters. For example, the other side may have better lawyers than the losing side. The other side may have friends among the jury or be friends with the judge. All of these things and more can easily lead to the loser in the court case having to pay an enormous judgment to either the winner or the state. If one is poor, then this can be something that easily destroys the meager foundation that the individual has painstakingly built over many years. And since the poor are always used as the punching bag of blame, everyone turns a blind eye to the injustice.

Hence, the strategy of becoming judgment proof. It is predominantly a defensive strategy against possible future debt, but it can also be a strategy of wealth preservation, especially if you currently face a great load of debt or several large judgments levied against you by a court. The strategy is quite simple: you want to trim down your assets and redirect them towards assets that are considered to be 'judgment proof' by the judicial system in which you currently live.

Each judicial system is different, and because of this, each and every one of you needs to independently research what the judicial system considers off-limits in terms of enforcing judgments. In the end, all debt becomes a 'judgment'; this is something that is worth keeping in mind, even if you do not have any intentions of pursuing a strategy that allows you to become judgment proof. And, of course, it must be said, becoming judgment proof requires many sacrifices, hence why it is predominantly a strategy for the very poor who wish to live the best financial life that they can.

The usual assets that a judicial system will consider to be judgment proof include the following: housing, transportation such as an automobile/truck/motorcycle, tools and equipment that are necessary for you to perform your career, and essential assets that are needed for life, for example, expensive medical equipment that is necessary for you to remain alive and healthy. Of course, this seems obvious, and that does not leave all that much room for 'non-essential' assets and amenities that can be seized, but if one is willing to modify their requirements for happiness, it is not bad at all.

Is it ideal that you should aim to only own things that are just the essentials? No. But that is the current system that we live under, and unless we change it, it is the system that we must plan for. Living a judgment-proof life is not the end of the world. You get to preserve your housing and means of transportation in nearly all cases, as well as the tools and equipment that are necessary for you to perform your career. This latter part is something that is vitally important, especially if you wish to live life to the fullest while pursuing a judgment-proof strategy.

For example, let us say that your current career is something that is terrible in every sense of the word. You work late hours, and each of these hours is backbreaking in terms of labor intensity. Your employer views you more as a piece of machinery than as a person, and your pay is paltry. To add insult to injury, you somehow drew the ire of a client who has deep pockets and is suing you repeatedly for reasons that are more or less frivolous, but still sufficiently grounded in reality that they are not thrown out by the court.

You end up losing one of the lawsuits, and the judgment that ends up being levied against you is immense. With several other pending lawsuits against you by the same individual, you see the writing on the wall, and you realize that your current life is more or less over.

You immediately begin to pursue a strategy of becoming judgment proof. You start to sell all of your assets that can be subject to judicial seizure, and you use the funds to pay down a significant amount of your mortgage. You pay off in full your automobile debt, and you decide that you want to pursue a new career that is more exciting. You use the last of your funds from liquidating your assets to purchase a very powerful computer, one of the best currently available on the market. You will need it for your new career as a graphic designer, something that you have always wanted to do.

With your judgment-proof strategy now enacted, your life begins to change, both for the better because of said strategy and for the worse because of the judgments. Since you now no longer care about your old job, you work inefficiently and without a care, and your employer ends up terminating you after a month.

You now focus full-time on your graphic design work. Naturally, you do not make all that much money since you are just beginning to develop a list of clients, and you end up defaulting on your enormous debts. You are sued, and that client of your ex-employer who, for whatever reason, has an axe to grind with you uses the judgment to compel you to sell all of your assets to pay the judgment that he won. You show the list of your current assets, and his face scowls with anger as he sees that everything that you own cannot be sold to pay for a judgment.

He tries to get you to sell the computer, saying that it is not necessary for the work that you do, but you counter by showing how the computer is needed for high-level graphic design work. If you were to downgrade the computer, then the quality of your finished product would decline, especially since you work with very high-resolution images that need serious computing power to process and create. The court agrees and rules the computer a necessary tool for your career. Your life is now in a very safe position. The worst that can happen now is a portion of your income every month is garnished for the repayment of the judgments that are currently levied against you.

View such income garnishments as another tax and wait until all the lawsuits are finished before filing for bankruptcy. Of course, file for bankruptcy only if the bankruptcy laws are the same as the judgment-proof laws, which they usually tend to be. Furthermore, remember that being judgment proof gives you many advantages. For example, remember that client of your ex-employer who just won't leave you alone? Feel free to spread the word about your story on social media, and laugh as the defamation lawsuits come pouring in. After all, even if you lose every single one, it won't matter because you are judgment proof. That immunity and freedom is something that is incredibly powerful and arguably the greatest benefit of the judgment-proof strategy.

Naturally, many will view such a lifestyle as that of a 'deadbeat,' and they will shame you. But what is more important to you? Is it social acceptance? Remember that many who seem to have it all worked out have such a life because of debt. The moment that the issuer of the debt comes to collect, and for whatever reason said individual cannot repay his debt, his life will come crashing down. Approval from such people is not all that important.

What is important, however, is the peace of mind that being judgment proof can give you. State-funded museums, parks, libraries, and other such amenity services are free of charge in most cases for local residents. Traveling on the cheap is also something that you can do. One can live a full and vibrant life without all that much wealth, so long as the stability of a solid foundation is there. With a stable foundation, you can rest easy and not worry as much.

This is what being judgment proof gives you. You will never be rich with this strategy; the moment that you accumulate too much wealth, it will be seized in order to pay for the judgments. But if you are willing to live an ascetic lifestyle and appreciate the things that do not need money, then it is a good strategy to finally obtain some peace of mind from your debt.

Suing The Issuer Of The Debt

The previous three chapters discussed different ways to avoid your debt: declaring bankruptcy, fleeing the country, or becoming judgment proof—all of these strategies are effective for escaping the chains of your debt. But sometimes, you want to take the fight directly to the source and demand that the chains be removed. This is where this chapter comes in.

We use the word 'suing' in a broad sense. There is the obvious suing of the lender in a court of law, but there are also alternative ways of confronting the lender to compel them to release the chains of your debt. Tactics like public perception and campaigning, where you paint the lender in a negative light, can compel said lender to forgive your debt willingly in the face of public pressure. Additionally, advocacy in the political sense can encourage politicians in your respective nation to modify laws to make your debt invalid, whether through forgiveness or by rendering your current debt terms illegal and thus null and void.

We'll start with suing. Unfortunately, many lenders are aware of the possibility of being sued, and because of this, they usually create ironclad contracts that negate the possibility of a successful lawsuit against them as much as possible. Most borrowers do not read the contracts in full since the vast majority of the hundreds of pages are filled with 'legal-speak,' which uses very specific vocabulary that can be quite confusing for those without a legal background. Typically, legal-speak ends up taking several hundred pages to convey a single sentence: "The terms of this contract cannot be changed through judicial proceedings."

Such legal-speak is effective, and many lawsuits end up failing. The fact that you cannot use the judicial system to get rid of the debt is one of the main tools that lenders use to compel you to repay it. You can utilize the nuclear bomb option of bankruptcy, but lenders know very well that it wipes out your finances completely, leaving you locked out of most credit services for at least five years. Luckily, there are other ways besides suing.

The main alternative is public perception and campaigning. This strategy is quite simple; since you cannot get the judicial system to clear your debt, you need to persuade the lender to willingly clear it for you. Of course, that is the last thing the lender wants to do. After all, the longer the debt is outstanding, the more money the lender earns through interest. Fortunately, you can 'encourage' the lender to clear the debt for you with the help of others.

Lenders fear two things: changes in the law and the broad masses. They fear changes in the law for one main reason: if the law changes, then the hundreds of pages of legal-speak, which were once ironclad against any potential lawsuits, suddenly become worthless. The broad masses, on the other hand, are feared for two reasons. The first reason is the ability of the masses to exert pressure on politicians to change the law. The second reason? The masses are all potential customers for the lenders.

If a specific lender has a negative public perception, competitors can easily capture the market share of the unpopular lender. Because of how interest works, if most of the masses do business with other lenders, they will become wealthier every single day, while the targeted lender is left increasingly behind. Catching up to a rival who has had years of interest as a head start is very difficult, if not impossible. Because of this, lenders do everything they can to portray themselves in a positive light.

For them, it is a delicate balance between high interest rates and fees, which are the bread and butter of their earnings, and public perception. Usually, they try to sell the benefits of their services. Borrowing to go to college and earn more money once you receive an education is one example. Borrowing to invest in the stock market or a business startup is another. The interest fees are only a small part of the earnings you can make with access to borrowed capital! That is the slogan and pitch that nearly all lenders use.

Let's assume, since such an assumption is true in the vast majority of cases, that your debt did not 'earn' you great returns as you thought. Perhaps your business venture failed, but the debt remains. Maybe you purchased stock right before a major market correction, but the debt is still there. Or perhaps, as is unfortunately so common, you borrowed money to pay for medical care, food, or housing. And of course, the debt is still there.

Naturally, the debt is an annoyance you want to eliminate as much as possible. The judicial system is out; the legal-speak in the contract all but guarantees that the lender would win any lawsuit. With the judicial system out as an option, especially since bankruptcy will destroy your current financial foundation, you need the help of the masses.

You need to share your story far and wide and disseminate it everywhere. Initially, you will encounter raw silence. No one is going to care since they hear these stories all the time. Naturally, if the lender hears about your story and complaints, they will ignore it. After all, responding will only add legitimacy to your grievances. This is where the vast majority of public perception campaigns fail. They start, receive only silence, and the person who initiated the campaign then gives up in despair. The lenders know this, and they are betting that you will give up just like everyone else. Of course, you are not going to give up; you are going to persist.

Since you are not being quiet, other individuals will start to pay attention. They will say: "He hasn't shut up for months; maybe he has something important to say?" They stop to listen to you, and most will just give an "eh, whatever" and walk away. Some will quit here and now; after all, spending months trying to get someone to listen to you, only to be brushed off once you finally get attention, stings deeply. But no matter how painful the sting, you deal with it and carry on with your task.

You have been patient, and you swore to yourself that you would carry on no matter the setbacks, and you finally start to see the fruit of your labor. A few who stopped to listen to your story tell you they have similar experiences to share. It is only a few people, downtrodden and under the burden of debt, just like you. Yet while many would see only empty support, you instead see great potential. You talk to all of these people and decide to combine your voices, amplifying each and every one into a mighty roar.

You, alongside these fellow debt sufferers, start a consumer and political advocacy organization. Using this organization, you begin to disseminate your stories far and wide across the country. More and more debt sufferers hear your message and ask to join your organization. Suddenly, you have hundreds of voices all yelling in unison against the lenders who will not lift the burden of debt from your shoulders.

The lenders were starting to get increasingly nervous, but they remained silent. "They will be an annoyance, but we still have new customers coming in, and eventually they'll run out of money or willingness to continue." That will be their logic, and in many cases, it is correct. Similar organizations have been formed in the past, only to disintegrate from drama within the organization and lack of enthusiasm as nothing seems to change. Yet this organization was different; more and more debt sufferers joined its ranks, and every day it grew in financial donations and in the intensity of its message. Many started to take notice, including the lenders.

The point was reached when the lenders could no longer remain silent, since potential customers were beginning to inquire about the 'terms' that the organization was contesting. The lenders targeted by the organization decided to coordinate and hit back with a counter-campaign. They dug for dirt on the leaders of the advocacy organization and, coupled with a detailed critique and mockery of the organization and the principles for which it stands, they unleashed a rebuttal against the advocacy organization. The lenders sat back and smiled; after all, there was no way the organization could hope to remain effective after such a move.

But it remained effective and increased the vitriol of the attacks against the lenders, especially after such a move. Many customers agreed, and for the first time, the beginnings of a broad coalition started to form against the lenders. The lenders tried everything, but eventually, they failed, and the coalition grew so large that politicians began to advocate for debt relief in order to win votes for their campaigns.

Public advocacy and political advocacy tend to be one and the same, especially once an organization or coalition grows large enough to obtain power. When you can't get the lenders to forgive the debt willingly, sometimes you need to use public influence and politics to get the job done. Because so many quit before they achieve the debt relief they seek, lenders prefer this system. It is incredibly dangerous for them if an organization grows large enough, but because of all the steps that one must take, the chances of such an event occurring are very small. The key to success in such an endeavor? Don't ever quit before the job is done.

Avoiding Debt

We've spent the entire book so far discussing what to do if you are in debt: get rid of it, negate it, or compel the lender to change the terms. The book has focused on dealing with debt once you have it. However, a vital part of the foundation of debt-busting is avoiding debt in the first place. After all, you do not need to deal with it if you never have it to begin with.

Avoiding debt involves two different strategies: the strategy of willpower and discipline, and the strategy of preparation. You need both strategies to stand the greatest chance of remaining debt-free. The strategy of willpower and discipline is straightforward: avoid entering debt by having the willpower and discipline to live within your means. The strategy of preparation helps you withstand unexpected tribulations that could leave you penniless if caught unprepared.

We start with the strategy of willpower and discipline. As mentioned earlier, it involves the strength to continue living within your income and not exceed it, even if you want to. Life, especially in a consumerist society, places considerable pressure on individuals to accumulate more possessions, consume more amenities, and be the best consumers they can be. Popularity among the masses is often measured by the level of consumption one can enjoy. If someone is wealthy and can afford extravagant foods, enjoy amenities that rival a year's salary, or purchase assets that are beyond the wildest dreams of someone earning an average income, then they are considered popular.

Everyone wishes to be accepted and popular, so they try their best to emulate the wealthy. They strive to "keep up with the Joneses." Unfortunately, if their income simply will not allow it, the only option to live beyond one's means is debt. For a time, this works magically and without fault. The debt is transformed into a small monthly payment to be repaid over several years or more. This small payment seems trivial; after all, you just need to cut down on a few basic amenities every month, and you will have enough to repay the debt eventually.

This is where everyone gets trapped. An automobile model that is well beyond the affordability of most people is easily justified as an expense if it is transformed into a small percentage of your monthly income. You can enjoy all the attention, positive status, and joy of driving such a car without having to pay anything upfront. "$200 a month for this car that would take decades to save for—those terms are acceptable!" And perhaps they are.

Of course, one cannot keep up with the Joneses with just a single car. There are other amenities that one must have to properly show off in a consumerist society. One particularly expensive debt in many Western nations is college debt. While I would not say that this is a frivolous expense—because education is never a negative—I would argue that a debt that grows to $20,000–$40,000 USD a year to attend the most prestigious university that money can buy is certainly frivolous. Much like the previous example, education is vital for a good life, just as an automobile is essential for transport. However, a cheap car and a solid education work just as well.

We will focus exclusively on this "purchase of prestige," especially if one wishes to attend a specific university even if financial assistance can be obtained for a more affordable option elsewhere. Remember, the reason these frivolous "amenities" are so easily justified as necessary expenses is that they are practical assets in part. A luxury BMW transports you from point A to point B. A college/university education enhances your knowledge and can open doors to new employment or business opportunities.

However, remember that a reliable used car or even a reasonably priced semi-used automobile can achieve the same goal: delivering you from point A to point B. Likewise, a less expensive college can teach you the same material as a college that costs several times more. Paying more for a product because it is considered "luxury" is a fool's errand. Always pay for inherent worth and usability when purchasing a service or commodity, not luxury.

Initially, debt may seem reasonable and affordable. There are many positive uses for debt; we will cover them in more detail in the upcoming chapter: "When Debt Can Be Beneficial for You." But for now, remember that debt may initially appear harmless. One can reasonably afford a small loan, especially if your income is stable. The issue arises when unexpected events cause your future to differ from what you imagined.

And just like that, the snare closes around your neck, and you start to choke on the debt you willingly incurred. For example, let's say you suddenly lose your job for any reason. You now have all these expenses to pay, plus the monthly debt obligation payments that are due. If you neglect these payments, you will incur fees and penalties in most cases. Your misery becomes the lender's gain, and you find yourself in a hole that is hard to escape.

Never forget this, reader: debt is the purchase of good moments from the future. Income and wealth you could earn later are transported back in time in the form of a lump sum principal and then repaid as debt. The problem with debt is the setbacks that can occur in the future. Since you are in debt and lack a financial cushion, a setback can quickly escalate into a chaotic disaster.

That is really all there is to avoiding debt. With the exception of severe setbacks caused by societal conditions, such as a medical event that leaves you in debt, willpower and a change of lifestyle, followed by a habit of saving, is a surefire way to avoid debt. While debt is never 100% unavoidable, you can do everything possible to minimize it by following the advice presented in this chapter.

There Is No Shame In Seeking Help

The last chapter discussed the best means by which an individual can avoid debt in the first place: willpower and a change of lifestyle, followed by a habit of saving. These aforementioned strategies are a surefire way to avoid debt. Of course, it is a surefire way to avoid debt caused by you, and not debt inflicted upon you by an outside force or a simple reality of life. While we touched on this subject before in this book, it is important enough that I feel it deserves a chapter of its own. Remember, reader, there is no shame in seeking help, especially if you struggle with debt.

We've mentioned this before as well, but it deserves to be reiterated: the only people who benefit from your shame are the lenders. If you are ashamed to seek help, then the only thing that will change is the difficulty in repaying and/or getting rid of your debt. The lender is still going to get every single cent of the principal plus interest that the contract specifies, and since you are too ashamed to get help, you will have to repay that principal plus interest all by yourself.

The help that you may need depends on your situation, but no matter the circumstances you may find yourself in, you can always use an additional opinion or observation from a trusted friend or individual. It may be embarrassing to admit that you have debt to this person, especially if they are a friend of many years, but temporary embarrassment is better than many years of slow misery as you pay it off by yourself.

A friend or trusted individual has many advantages. They may give you a loan that covers the remaining high-interest balance, and instead of a high-interest rate, they may only charge you a low interest, or perhaps no interest at all. The fact that you are good friends means you can focus on repaying the loan as quickly as possible, all while saving many hundreds if not thousands of dollars in interest. Had you never consulted this friend, this option of 'switching' the debt would have never been available to you.

There is another advantage to admitting that you have a debt problem to this friend or trusted individual. Let's say that the debt you are trying to repay just keeps growing, and you are not knowledgeable about debt, so you have no idea why the balance continues to go up instead of down. After admitting that you have a debt problem to this individual, they take a look at the debt contract and find something disturbing.

It turns out that the contract you signed is predatory, so much so that there is a good chance you can get the contract thrown out in court or terminated by the lender with sufficient public outrage in your favor! Your trusted individual tells you to contact the lender and see if you can get the contract terminated with their consent. You, after all, paid an enormous amount of predatory interest, and it is in the lender's interest to break off the contract now that the unjust terms have been discovered.

Naturally, the lender refuses. You then decide to contact a local news organization, at the same time as contacting a local lawyer with knowledge in debt contracts and negotiations. The local news organization, after reviewing the evidence you showed them in the form of the contract and your interview, decides that this is a story worth covering and airs it. The publicity from this local news organization, combined with the pro bono lawyer you've just obtained, gives you two great advantages.

The judge agrees with your side, and the contract is thrown out. But that is not all. Since the lender took advantage of your financial illiteracy, the court decided that you were to be awarded financial compensation from the lender as damages. Not only did talking to your friend and/or trusted advisor prove beneficial in getting out of debt, but you made money! The settlement was a sizable amount, covering all of the interest and a portion of the principal that you paid the lender, plus extra!

Everything we just mentioned would have never been possible if you had decided to keep your 'shameful' situation silent and under wraps. You would have suffered in silence, paying off a loan with terrible interest rates that are on the level of usury. No one can fault you in the end for looking for help; after all, in the above example, asking others for help allowed you to not only clear your debt but earn money on top!

Those who are most likely to shame you for seeking help, the ones who will say things like: "You made the bed; now you get to lie in it!", "If you do not like the terms of the debt, then you should not have signed on the dotted line!", and "Only a loser can't repay his debts," are people who are irrelevant. Listening to them will not make your current burdens any easier; it will only make them harder. Since they are useless to you in helping make your life better, the same value should be attributed to their opinions.

Remember, reader, the knowledge contained in this book cannot do a thing to help you if you let shame get in the way. The advice in this book can be controversial; in a few cases, especially with the 'little lie' example regarding the bankruptcy court, it can be illegal in certain judicial jurisdictions. In the end, however, the information and knowledge presented to you here in this book are given to you in a state of inertness. Knowledge by itself is useless without action to accompany it. You can read this book, as well as a hundred other books regarding debt and how to get out of it. But if you let shame get in the way, it was all for nothing.

Most Common Sources of Debt

Following on the heels of the previous chapter, we have a chapter that summarizes, as well as further clarifies, the most common sources of debt. Repeating the knowledge that has already been mentioned is important because the reader should never forget the sources of debt, especially the most common ones. If you avoid the sources of debt, then you don't get into debt; it is that simple.

We have the sources that can be considered under the 'consumer' camp. These involve debts that originate directly as a result of the desire to consume goods, services, and other amenities. They include credit card debt and merchant credit line debt. The merchant credit line debt is rapidly becoming extinct in most consumerist economies, being replaced by the ubiquitous credit card issued by banking institutions due to consumer convenience and changes in lending regulation laws. Since merchant credit line debt is more or less a credit card issued by a specific merchant, we will fold it into the broader credit card debt discussion.

Credit cards are incredible little things. They have allowed the act of purchasing to progress to new levels that we could have never imagined. We have gone from the old form of currency notes and coins of yesteryear to the new and present form of immediate exchange. They allow for more economic wealth to be produced due to the ease of purchase and payment for both the consumer and the merchant, and they enable banking institutions to earn more money by charging interest on credit card balances, as well as fees from each transaction.

But just as much as they are great tools for making purchasing easier, they can also be terrible little things that destroy not only your credit but your financial life as well. It is no secret that credit cards have some of the worst interest rates of any loan in existence, ranging from roughly 14% for those with good credit all the way to 30%-40% for those with terrible credit.

In the modern age, credit cards tend to be the most common source of debt; hence, we will start with them first. They are the kings of the consumer debt camp in terms of sources of debt. They are easy to use, convenient, and nice to have, but they also allow temptation to win the day. If one has cash in hand, you see the notes leave your hand as you purchase the commodity; you effectively can see the loss that you must endure to obtain the good or service that you are purchasing. With the credit card, however, all you need to do is swipe, insert, or tap it.

That's it. No matter the size of the purchase, and thus the loss of currency notes that you must endure to purchase said good or service, it feels the same each and every time you use your card. Furthermore, the notes themselves are not removed from your person; you still have the same number of notes as you did previously. If you have a habit of constantly checking your bank account, you will see that the balance remains the same. The only thing that changed was your debt obligation, which increased by an amount equal to the price of the good or service that you just purchased.

Following the credit cards, we have the second most common source of debt in the consumer debt camp; you could say that it is the queen of the consumer debt camp. These are the 'reward' incentives. They can come in many forms; for example, many credit cards have them. Rewards like cashback, frequent flyer miles, or 'points' that can be redeemed for rewards are all examples of reward incentives. These can be very beneficial, as well as very destructive to your finances.

Rewards incentives are as common as the air you breathe in consumerist economies. They are the lubricant that helps keep everything moving. Just about anything can be considered a reward incentive, even the 25% off sales that seem to never end. The entire point of a reward incentive is to get you to spend your money on something you otherwise would not. If something is on sale, then there is a greater chance that you will buy it. If something gives you a reward, then you are more likely to buy it since you get the item as well as the reward in exchange for your money.

It can even be used to get you to spend using a certain method, such as a credit card. The credit card can offer you rewards each time you purchase goods and services with it, all in order to get you to use it more often. It is very effective; the credit card rewards programs, as well as the convenience of loans and not having to carry cash, are why the credit card rose to dominance in the financial world.

Following the consumerist sources of debt, which you can largely control with sufficient willpower and acceptance of living within your means, you have the institutional forms of debt. These forms of debt arise when you have to pay for a specific good or service that simply cannot be ignored, but you lack the funds to do so. The sources of debt depend on the institution you live under; some are notorious for being a fountain of debt for the residents living under them, while others do their best to minimize any and all sources of institutional debt.

We start with fundamental institutional debt; this is debt needed to purchase essential goods and services for life. Medical debt, college/university debt, and debt for the acquisition of food, water, and shelter all fall under fundamental institutional debt. Avoiding these debts is difficult; while educational debt such as college/university debt is optional in some regard, the others are not. After all, you can live without a college degree, but you will not live without necessary medical care, or food, water, and shelter.

The other debt can be classified under the broad category of institutional debt. This is similar to the previous category of fundamental institutional debt, with the only exception that these institutional debts do not fall under essential for life. Most forms of institutional debt have the effect of knocking you down a few pegs in terms of class. This is especially borne by the 'middle' classes of the respective institution and economy, who have to deal with the full force of the debts while lacking the necessary asset and money cushion that the upper classes have to withstand them.

Forms that this debt can take tend to be in the realm of fees or taxes levied upon you by the institutional state that you live under. Most institutions are transparent about the possibility of you having to suffer these fees or taxes. In the case of fees, such as the registration of an automobile or the usage of a specific publicly owned good such as railway transportation or a national park, the fees will be posted clearly. In other cases, the information may be hidden.

Taxation tends to be either overt or covert. Overt taxation is commonly found in cases where the general public does not see the taxation as a problem. For example, in many jurisdictions, the taxation of property will be overt. The property is worth a certain amount, whether it be land, farm yield, or residence, or any combination of the three, and due to this amount of value, a specific levy of monthly, quarterly, or yearly tax is due to the state.

Covert taxation, however, can be anywhere, even in areas where it seems to be all but invisible. Usually, this comes in two main forms: hidden taxation that is built into the price of a specific good or service, or direct taxation of the currency that is being used in the economy. Covert taxation is the best strategy for a government that wants to slowly change the economic behavior of its population with as little 'inefficiency' as possible.

All debts originate when the individual in question, who becomes the debtor, cannot pay for something. After all, if you had the money to pay for the respective good and/or service, then you would not need to go into debt in the first place. Because of this truth, it is important to keep an eye out for the covert forms of taxation, as they can and will put pressure on you that, more often than not, leads to entering debt.

For example, let's start with the first of the two main forms of covert taxation: hidden taxation built into the price of a specific good or service. This tends to come in a few different forms, but the main ones include the following: VAT, corporate income tax, sin tax, and finally sales tax, which is built into the price instead of being levied at checkout.

VAT tends to be a form of taxation often seen in European countries or nations within the British Commonwealth. It effectively serves as a sales tax on the respective 'evolutions' of a good or service through the production economy. To help illustrate this concept further, let us use an automobile. Here is a specific good that requires many different individual goods to produce, each of which must travel through several evolutions in the production economy to become the individual goods that are, in turn, used to construct the automobile.

The chassis of the automobile is made of a strong material that provides strength and support to the entire automobile while also being lightweight to help with fuel economy. In the modern age, it tends to be either aluminum or some sort of specialized plastic mixture that often contains metal. Whatever the case may be regarding the material composition of the chassis, it goes through many different evolutions in the production economy.

To make it simple, let's assume that the chassis is made of metal. To make it even simpler, it is just a single metal; let's say that it is aluminum. Aluminum goes through many different evolutions in the production economy, and during each evolution, VAT is charged. We start with the mine. Aluminum-containing ores are mined, packed into mine carts, and wheeled out. In this specific case, the mine sells the raw ore to a smelter.

Here we find the first VAT payment. For the sake of simplicity, we will say that it is 10%. This is usually paid by the purchaser, and the mine sells the ore to the smelter for the price that is agreed upon, plus the 10% VAT. Now, VAT itself can be made into a covert tax even at this stage. For example, the respective government or state that is levying the VAT in the first place could decide to make it illegal for VAT to be collected at the point of sale; it instead must be paid by the seller as a portion of sales.

In this case, the mine either absorbs the VAT or raises the price in order to compensate. Whatever the case may be, VAT is paid either by the seller or the buyer. Returning to the discussion on the automobile chassis, we left off with the purchase of the ore by the smelter. The smelter then smelts the ore into raw aluminum chassis blocks. For the sake of convenience, this specific smelter also serves as the refiner, but you can easily have the refiner refine the ore into aluminum ingots and then sell those ingots to the smelter, which will incur a VAT charge.

And so on, until the evolutions result in parts that can be used to construct an automobile. Each evolution, from the ore all the way to the final part, results in a VAT tax. Why is this information important? It is important because much of what the state does tends to trickle down and more often than not results in a greater possibility of you entering debt.

It pays to be vigilant, especially if you are someone who is busy saving wealth to avoid debt in the future. If the state you live under is proving to be irresponsible in its stewardship of the economy, then you must prepare beforehand. Debt results from either sudden and unavoidable financial costs that exceed one's reserves or from financial irresponsibility. Since the state itself is the primary cause of either a prosperous or ruinous economy, you should always keep an eye on it, much the same way you keep an eye on your spouse.

When Debt Can Be Beneficial For You

All throughout this book, we've been sounding the alarm about the perils of debt. We've mentioned over and over again the different strategies that you can use to get out of debt, and we've been more or less consistent in portraying debt as the worst ball and chain that you can have around your neck. However, in this chapter, we are going to take a slight break from all of that. In this chapter, we are going to talk about the different situations when debt can be beneficial for you, instead of problematic.

Debt is the borrowing of money. This definition is obvious and commonly known. However, the act of borrowing money opens several possibilities, some of which can be beneficial for you.

We start with the ability to use capital to make money, the most obvious and well-known of the different positive situations that debt can put you in. This path is quite clear, and exploiting it for your benefit is simple. You take the capital that debt gives you and use it to generate a return on your investment.

Usually, the best investment tends to be a business enterprise, specifically the establishment of a new business. The second-best investment tends to be the purchase of already existing business enterprises, either completely or partially through the purchase of business stocks. Finally, the third-best investment is the utilization of the capital obtained through debt to pay down other debts, particularly those with worse terms and interest rates.

The issue, however, and the reason why this 'short break' of a chapter is indeed so short, is the following. Debt adds unpredictability, akin to breaking the wall of your house in order to get a piece of wood that is needed for kindling a fire. Yes, you get the piece of wood, and you get it instantly, without having to go outside with an axe and cut it down from a still-standing tree.

But your wall now has a chunk of wood missing, and no doubt the violent process by which you removed said piece of wood has left cracks all around the injury. If this is the first and last time that you remove a piece of wood from your wall, you should be fine. Other than an ugly wall and perhaps a slight draft from the outside, you won't suffer any problems from your amateur attempt at wall surgery. If, however, you make this wood-gathering strategy a habit, then you will very quickly find yourself with a wall that'll collapse against the slightest breeze.

Money is wood, and to heat your life, oftentimes you need wood to start a fire. Entering debt in order to heat your life is akin to ripping out wood chunks from your wall to start a fire. It'll help get the ball rolling on heating your life, but it is a dangerous game. If your wall collapses, there is nothing stopping the winter air that will soon descend upon your humble abode.

The Importance of Busting Debt Before Anything Else

As we near the end of this book, we will finish with a combination of both a recap and supplementary material for things we have already covered, as well as new material in case we have not. If you have read this book from the beginning, you are now ready to bust your debt; this final part is to ensure that you do it well and with style.

This chapter will primarily be a recap. After all, the point of having to bust your debt before you worry about anything else regarding your financial situation has been emphasized throughout this book. Still, just in case the point has not taken root in your brain, we will review the necessity of busting debt before anything else one final time.

As has been said previously, debt is the ball and chain around your neck. It is the hole that gets deeper and deeper the longer you are in it. It is the worst thing you can have for your financial health. It serves to take away wealth and opportunity from the future to provide capital today. Sometimes it is good; we briefly covered in the previous chapter the cases where debt can be beneficial. But even when it is beneficial, debt comes at a price, and it is often a price that you never want to pay if you can help it.

Interest does not go away. The terms of the debt, which you gave legitimacy and power to when you signed on that dotted line, do not go away. The debt remains until you get rid of it. You can get rid of it through the termination of the debt contract itself, getting it voided by a court, or by the lender. You can also get rid of it by paying the entire outstanding balance, in which case the contract is completed, and the fees and interest fade away into nothingness.

But if you do not get rid of the debt, whether by voiding the contract or paying off the outstanding balance, then problems occur. In most market economies, where a specific currency or bundle of currencies is used to purchase goods and services, money is the lifeblood. With money, you can purchase goods and services; the more money you have, the better your financial status and, frankly, your status at large in society.

If you have debt, you are effectively slowly bleeding. Your blood, the money you need to survive in such a system, is being slowly drained in the form of interest and fees. These interests and fees mean that you have less and less blood in your veins, blood that could possibly be useful in some future circumstance that you currently have no idea about.

It is this reality that makes busting debt the most important thing—something you should do before anything else. Debt makes you weaker in the financial sense and also weaker in terms of resisting unfavorable deals. There is a reason why many sensitive government positions require you to have little to no debt as a condition of obtaining your security clearance. Not only is there the moral dilemma—whether you have the willpower and temperament to be trusted with such sensitive knowledge—but there is also the issue of being weak in terms of manipulation resistance.

After all, if you have debt, some third party wishing to obtain the sensitive knowledge you have access to can use your debt as leverage. This third party can offer to give you the money needed to pay off your debt, or it can threaten to disclose the existence of your perilous financial situation to the public at large. Either way, the fact that you are in debt makes you vulnerable—a fact that those who may entrust you with sensitive secrets know all too well, hence why they ask.

The same is true for financial institutions. If you are in debt, how can you be trusted to give solid financial advice to clients at large? Furthermore, as is the case with the sensitive government position mentioned above, what is the chance that a third party can take advantage of your current situation and use your weakness against you in pursuit of gain?

Finally, the importance of busting your debt is not just in the financial situation. Not only is it quite obvious and has been mentioned extensively throughout this book, but it is not the most important reason. No, the most important reason—the reason why you should focus exclusively on busting your debt before you focus on anything else—is quite simple: peace of mind.

Debt brings stress to your life. You want to get rid of it, and your mind races as it thinks of the different ways to do just that. You start to worry because you know that this debt, and the actions you need to take to pay it down or get rid of it, are going to be costly. They will require effort—effort that will come at the expense of effort applied elsewhere—and they will require time, time that you are never going to get back.

It is not only money that is at stake; you can always earn back money, but you can never earn back time. The specific minute of the specific hour of the specific day in the respective specific year will never occur again. The day you were born is a day that will never occur again, as will the day you die. All the days in between will never occur again.

The longer you allow your debt to exist, to continue enforcing its contract obligations of fees and interest, the longer it will take you to get rid of it, whether by repaying the outstanding balance or by voiding the contract. All of that time and effort is time and effort that you will never get back, and it is time and effort that could undoubtedly be applied elsewhere.

A quote that is often cited, and one you have more than likely already heard, is the following: "The borrower is slave to the lender." This is a powerful quote; its power is one reason why it is so often used in conversation, after all. It is a quote of truth and simplicity. It tells us everything we need to know in only seven words.

If you are in debt, your future, at least in part, is owned by someone else—your lender. You cannot do certain things because you lack the funds to do them. Why do you lack the funds? Because you are in debt, and you must pay back not only the balance but all the interest and fees that come with it.

Opportunities that could have been pursued must be ignored; doors that could have been opened are instead closed shut. You have to work and labor to pay the debt balance and the interest and fees, even if you do not want to. Why? Because you are in debt. Working without consent for the betterment of someone else is the very definition of slavery.

Before anything else, you need to get out of debt. There is no excuse that can change this fact. You cannot be free if you are a slave; to stop being a slave, you need to get out of debt. Focus on nothing else.

Find Ways to Transfer Your Expenses to the State

Here we have an interesting chapter, one that is perfectly positioned near the end of the book. At first glance, the title may appear to be a repeat of the previous lesson given all the way back in the chapter titled "Becoming Judgment Proof," where you attempt to live without any assets, effectively negating any possibility of debt enforcement against your person. But no, this chapter is somewhat different—similar, yes, but different.

This chapter discusses transferring your expenses to the state in terms of business and life. The fewer expenses you have, the less likely you will find yourself in debt, provided that you have sufficient willpower and financial stewardship to avoid debt due to rash consumerism. You are effectively looking for a subsidy for your respective lifestyle: have the state pay your expenses so that you can save more money and, because of that, be better off financially and more resilient to future shocks that may occur.

You may be thinking: "So go on welfare?" No, it is not that simple. First and foremost, welfare tends to have stringent income and asset restrictions; it is, after all, designed for the poorest individuals in society. While it is perfectly adequate as an assistant to the individual who wants to live the judgment-proof lifestyle, it is not helpful at all to the individual with income and assets.

For this individual, who will not qualify for welfare because of his income and assets, options are more limited. But just because you cannot get on welfare does not mean that the state cannot help ease your expenses. After all, the state is created by the hand of man; if it can be created by the hand of man, it can certainly be changed by the hand of man.

The path toward transferring your expenses to your respective state in question will be different for each individual. Everyone has their own financial circumstances, and we all live in different countries, each with different states and means of doing things. However, most states have certain means by which you can transfer your expenses to the state. Here is one excellent example, which is obvious when you point it out, but it tends to hide in plain sight.

I will be using the United States as the respective government state for my example, but this path tends to be similar all across the planet. What is this path that I am talking about? Military service, more specifically a military career. If the obvious is not yet staring you in the face, I'll explain further.

The United States is a very developed country with regard to its economic infrastructure. For the accumulation of wealth, there is no equal in terms of cultural, state, and economic support. Other countries come close, but they usually lack in terms of cultural and state support regarding the individualistic pursuit of wealth. However, this generous attitude toward an individual accumulating wealth comes at a price: the relentless hatred for the individual who, for whatever reason, cannot accumulate wealth.

This is why the welfare systems of the United States pale in comparison to even lesser-developed economic countries. The European Union does not have the same generosity regarding individual wealth accumulation as the United States does, but the welfare system of the European Union is far superior to that of the United States.

Returning to our example of military service as a strategy for transferring your expenses to the state, we have an interesting result. For a nation that despises the subsidy of welfare, in whatever form it may occur, it certainly turns a blind eye to the welfare of the military, especially the welfare of those who work and serve under its banner.

Firstly, there is a clear distinction between the enlisted and officer corps in terms of this welfare, but only in certain parts. Regarding the welfare itself, it is massive, on a scale that will astonish those who take a seat and view it objectively, at least compared to the "welfare" of the general population or the work benefits of other careers outside of the military.

For example, one of the main platforms of socialism is the three universals: universal housing, universal education, and universal healthcare. This also tends to be the platform of social democracy, but I use the socialism ideology in this example because of the more negative connotations across society, especially in the United States.

If one were to argue that everyone who lives in the United States should have the right to housing, education, and healthcare, at the very least as part of their employment package, you'd be yelled at by a great swath of the population: "Get a better job, you lazy bastard!" This will be their reply after you propose such a thing, as well as dozens of other replies that are not dissimilar from each other. They will all, however, be negative.

Of course, in the military, things are somewhat different. This job, even for the lowliest of the enlisted, comes with the right to housing, in the form of a barracks/bunk for the enlisted, the right to education, in the form of the GI Bill and drill/military training, and finally the right to healthcare, in the form of Tricare. For those in the United States who fear socialism around every corner, it has taken root firmly in the military.

Naturally, you will get a response that will more or less be the following: "The military is a dangerous job; they deserve higher pay!" A decent argument in terms of fairness of compensation, it, however, falls flat when you compare, say, a military IT specialist who maintains a computer server in a military facility stateside with a fast-food worker. That IT specialist who is on active duty still gets the wonderful trinity of housing, education, and healthcare, and suffers less danger than the fast-food worker.

After all, how many knife cuts and stove burns is the IT worker going to get on the job? Either way, we've steered off course quite enough; the example of the military being a great strategy to transfer your expenses to the state has hopefully been explained well. There is no welfare involved, at least not in the traditional poverty safety net concept of welfare, and the military IT specialist we used in the above example has a great majority of his or her expenses taken care of by the government.

We will end with the above example, but there are many different strategies that you can pursue in order to transfer your life expenses over to the state. The important thing is to be vigilant; the above example is obvious, but only once it is pointed out. There are many more examples like the one above out there if you know where to look.

Encourage Broad Resistance to Current Debt Terms

This chapter, in a way, piggybacks on the previous one. The concept of transferring your expenses to the state, instead of paying for them yourself, can be augmented with broad popular support. If the general culture and society view the transferring of expenses to the state as a grave sin, then the state will likely do everything it can to prevent you from doing so. This can be seen somewhat in the United States, where, unless you are in the military or otherwise wealthy and powerful enough to obtain government contracts, assistance from the state is viewed as the gravest of sins.

To best follow the lessons from the previous chapter, you need to establish broad support across society for resisting the current debt terms, in other words, the status quo. To do this, you need to encourage a widespread resistance to current debt terms among the general population. Without it, you'll be attacked by others as you seek to improve your life.

We've covered general principles for encouraging broad support previously in this book, so this will serve as a reminder and refresher in most respects. However, it is easier to have people agree to change the system for the better than to have them sympathize with a particular injustice that you are currently facing. It is an unfortunate reality of the world, but it is so.

Fortunately, when the same injustice that ails you also ails another, you have a common enemy. Encouraging others to oppose this common enemy is much easier than encouraging them to oppose your own enemy, which hurts no one else but yourself.

The first step is to illustrate the problem and present it in such a way that all who suffer from it can clearly understand both what they are suffering from and how to fix it. This is done through relentless propaganda and reporting, by ensuring that the issue is highlighted clearly, and then the message needs to be repeated again and again until everyone knows it.

Once this is done, the message needs to be maintained against the inevitable rebuttal that one is likely to receive from the lenders and the system at large. The status quo will fight until its last breath to ensure that things remain as they are; no system likes to be forced to change, especially when the change is as drastic as the modification of how debt works in a respective society.

Remember, reader, you can do everything right, follow all of the advice that this book gives you, have ironclad willpower regarding spending, and avoid debt like it's the plague. You can do all of that and still be wiped out if you face $1 million in medical debt. The debt terms and the way that the system works are the problem. Encouraging others to join you in fixing it; that is the solution to said problem.

Make Plans To Ensure Debt Never Appears Again

And finally, we have the second-to-last chapter of this book. This chapter is going to be very short because it contains just one single lesson: "The best way to make plans to ensure that debt never appears again is to read this book and remember its lessons." It is that simple.

So long as certain strategies outlined in this book are not problematic for you with regard to your individual system of morality, this book is a suit of metal armor for your finances. Whatever the situation—whether it is brutal debt, so severe that at first glance there appears to be no escape, or minor debt that just needs a little bit of elbow grease to eliminate—this book will teach you the strategies to deal with it.

Naturally, some specific examples may have been forgotten, which is why it is recommended to reread the book, especially the specific chapters that contain examples closest to your respective financial situation. Reread it often because this book has all the plans you need to ensure that debt never appears again in your life.

Closing Thoughts

We have arrived at the final chapter. Here we will discuss a few closing thoughts that will serve as the polish to the cornerstone of busting your debt, not only for this very moment but for all time.

As mentioned in the previous chapter, rereading this book to recall specific lessons is recommended, as is rereading it from time to time in the future. In addition to this book, keep your eyes and ears open for any stories regarding debt, whether in your immediate friends and family circle or beyond. These stories can involve someone entering debt, which can inform you of what you should avoid doing, or they can be about a new development in the legal world of debt contracts.

For example, if there is growing discontent with non-dischargeable debts in bankruptcy in your country, then you may wish to avoid aggressive repayment of your current outstanding balance, since the chances of a nationwide debt pardon increase the more that people are angered over the debt. Similarly, if your nation plans to collect non-dischargeable debts in bankruptcy more aggressively, then it is a good idea to either dust off your second passport, find a job that can provide residency in another country, or accelerate your plans to marry your significant other who has residency in another country.

In the end, however, what truly matters is achieving peace of mind. The worst part of debt is not the loss of money and assets that it often brings, especially if you allow it to sit and slowly fester. Yes, the loss of money and assets stings, and it can sting badly, but it is not the worst part of debt. The worst part of debt is the stress and the lack of peace of mind. Remember, every second that you spend in a moment of stress is a second wasted, which could have otherwise been enjoyed in a moment of relaxation or bliss.

Furthermore, every second that passes in your life is a second you will never get back. You can recover money and assets; such things come and go in life. But you will never get back the time you spend. Everyone spends it in the same amount, and we all, no matter how much wealth we may have, can never reclaim it.

This is the true tragedy of debt. It forces us to spend our seconds, our minutes, and our hours in stress and agony. These are the treasures we can never regain, the true losses that debt takes away from us. Never forget this, reader: one can be happy with no money or assets, but if you are miserable, then you are losing, no matter how much money or assets you may have. Bust debt before it busts your happiness.

Don't miss out!

Visit the website below and you can sign up to receive emails whenever Paul Haedo publishes a new book. There's no charge and no obligation.

https://books2read.com/r/B-A-CYJN-IGURB

BOOKS2READ

Connecting independent readers to independent writers.

Also by Paul Haedo

Peacekeeper Series
Peacekeeper: Prequel
Peacekeeper
Rising Tide
Star Rising
Star Destroyer

Proletarian Hearts Series
Proletarian Hearts: Part One

Sci-Fi Box Sets
Sci-Fi Novel Mega Pack: Five Standalone Stories
Peacekeeper: The Complete Series

Standalone Erotic Stories
Innocent Pilgrim

Standalone Literary Novels
Scandinavian Tequila: A Novel

Standalone Poetry Anthologies

Haedian Poetry: Volume One

Moments Are Butterflies: A Poetry Collection

Standalone Religion, Philosophy, and Politics Books

The Communist Republic

A Dalliance Across Thought

The Word Of Era

A Man's Guide To Surviving Marriage In The 21st Century

Marxist-Haedoism

White Assimilation

Peaceful Resistance

The Reality

Standalone Romance Novels

The Director

A Chance Encounter

Beauty Unexpected

Standalone Sci-Fi Novels

Future's Guardian

Journey Home

The Designer

Pulses

World Engine

The Mycelial Invasion

Emily Reed And The Humans

Standalone Sci-Fi Short Story Anthologies

Haedian Sci-Fi Short Stories: Volume One

Haedian Sci-Fi Short Stories: Volume Two

Standalone Self-Help Books

Stack It Tall: A Guide To Writing

Debt Buster: Free Yourself From The Shackles In Less Than A Year

Watch for more at https://books2read.com/ap/n7evX1.

About the Author

Paul Haedo is an author, poet, philosopher, and all-around free spirit, who enjoys the twin joys of writing and reading in his spare time. Paul believes that there is no limit to the number of genres and topics that one can read and write about. An all-around reader and author is something to aspire to according to him, not shy away from.

Such a sentiment is reflected all throughout Paul's total body of work. It is reflected in the many topics that he writes about, in the different arguments that he proposes, and in the worlds that he creates. No matter the topic, or the book, Paul tackles it just the same, with an intense passion for wisdom, and a great desire to see others share in the wisdom and joy of reading and writing.

Read more at https://books2read.com/ap/n7evX1.

www.ingramcontent.com/pod-product-compliance
Lightning Source LLC
LaVergne TN
LVHW090429210926
848480LV00002B/756
* 9 7 9 8 2 0 1 0 2 9 3 6 4 *